Soul You
Vol. IV

SCRIBBLE JOURNAL

Soul You Vol. IV: Scribble Journal. Copyright 2021 by Sherika Frazier Duncan. All rights reserved. No part of this publication may be reproduced, distributed, or transmitted in any form or by any means, including photocopying, recording, or other electronic or mechanical methods, without the prior written permission of the publisher, except in the case of brief quotations embodied in critical reviews and certain other noncommercial uses permitted by copyright law. For permission requests, write to the publisher, addressed "Attention: Permissions Coordinator," 3819 Ulmer Court, Tallahassee, FL 32311.

Sherika Duncan books may be purchased for educational, business or sales promotional use. For information, please email the Sales Department at sales@sherikaduncan.com.

First Edition Printed, February 2021
Library of Congress Cataloging-in-Publication Data has been applied for.
ISBN: 978-1-7364355-3-3

Table of Content

Your contract between you and the universe to manifest your good intentions of a healthy and successful life.

Call to Action 1

Quick Tips & Takeaways 2

Journaling to Creating a Better You 3

Journaling for Creativity and Inspiration 11

Journaling to Record Your Daily Routine 13

Journaling for Evolving into the Best You 14

Call to Action

Can you remember when you sat by a stream or the ocean and listened to the vibration of the water splattering against the rocks or seashells?

Did it make you feel at peace inside?

Based on the things we will notice every day; we will begin to embrace our writing exercises. Also, it will become a routine as we became more aware of our surroundings and thought patterns.

As we begin living in the moment daily, Our minds are always thinking or aware of something, like passing thoughts or worries or anxiety. Let's take the time to ponder our judgment behind these thoughts, fears, and concerns.

Don't know what to do? Use Google because you're not the first person in the entire galaxy that has struggled with the same issues and gets inspired by others.

Scribble your vision about your desired lifetime achievements on paper and be specific with the details. You should declare the goal, timeframe, and travel experiences to see it come to pass also a range of desired income.

Quick Tips & Takeaways

Make transparent whatever you aspire.
- Request the universe concerning it.
- Act (assist the universe; create opportunities).
- Believe in the plan; (set out good intentions).
- Recognize your discovery along the way; (take it all in).
- Raise your aura frequency.
- Remove every doubt and blockage.

There are a few essential areas to ensure success for you to attain your goals. Scribble down three things to bring you closer to your dream today. Visualize the conditions to aligning your current surroundings with your goals. *Lastly, try not to lose focus on every aspect of your dreams.*

Journaling to creating a better you

What type of life do you want to lead, short or long term?

Who are some of the people, places, and things to complement this vision?

What type of emotions do you think will this vision bring to your life?

_____

_____

_____

_____

What do you taste, smell, see, and hear with this vision in your five senses?

_____

_____

_____

_____

The unique setup abundance mindset is the answer to manifestation within your subconscious belief system by eliminating a poverty mindset.

How do you manifest these dreams in your life?
What would it take to achieve your dream life?

_____

_____

_____

_____

The road-map of manifestation, taking charge of our lives, transforming dreams into reality. The manifestation journey includes vision boards, goal setting, bullet journals; these are pieces to the puzzle. We must line out the path to manifestation by adding some tools to use at each point.

What type of feelings would you want to experience in this life every day?

_____

_____

_____

_____

_____

What are some of the things or experiences do you think to allow you to feel that way?

_____

_____

_____

_____

_____

How does limitations affect your choices and behaviors?

_____

_____

_____

_____

_____

How will you feel once the wish is fulfilled?

_____

_____

_____

_____

_____

Imagine all the sensations you will feel by materializing your dreams into a reality.

Will you talk, walk, look, think, feel or dress differently? Explain

_____

_____

_____

_____

Celebrate other accomplishments because doing so will inspire you. List three to four people you are inspired by.

_____

_____

_____

_____

Emotional Assessment	**Yes**	**No**

Place a check mark under

	Yes	No
Are you mostly a happy person?	☐	☐
Are you easily irritated?	☐	☐
Do you make contributions?	☐	☐
Do you feel valued for your contributions?	☐	☐
Are your relationships satisfying?	☐	☐
Do you cherish your relationships?	☐	☐
Are you achieving your personal goals?	☐	☐
Do you have a sense of worth and well-being?	☐	☐
Are you responsible for your actions?	☐	☐
Do you feel attractive?	☐	☐

What are your active obligations? What are you assigned to do? (for example, school volunteer, charity event organizer, football coach, babysitter, electrician).

_____
_____
_____
_____
_____

What are your aspirations? (for example, travel to Paris, start a charity fundraiser, lose weight, and get married).

_____
_____
_____
_____
_____

JOURNALING FOR CREATIVITY AND INSPIRATION

Translate how to visualize inspiration and ideas to describe your abilities or talents you possess.
Are you a great problem solver, a talented artist very supportive?

_____

_____

_____

_____

_____

_____

Recognize anything stands in the way of reaching your goals.

You can start by writing out positive affirmations to transfer your found weaknesses into success. Let's begin manifesting to create a better you by writing down a list of twelve positive "I am" statements concerning your life.

I am _____

I am _____

I am _____

I am _____

I am _____

I am _____

I am _____

I am _____

I am _____

I am _____

I am _____

I am _____

JOURNALING TO RECORD YOUR DAILY ROUTINE

Plan & Review Your Day Log Entries	
Date:	Plan: what good things do I plan to do today?
Review: what did I accomplish today?	
Date:	Plan: what good things do I plan to do today?
Review: what did I accomplish today	
Date:	Plan: what good things do I plan to do today?
Review: what did I accomplish today?	
Date:	Plan: what good things do I plan to do today?
Review: what did I accomplish today?	
Date:	Plan: what good things do I plan to do today?
Review: what did I accomplish today?	
Date:	Plan: what good things do I plan to do today?
Review: what did I accomplish today?	

Journaling for Evolving into the Best You

The Transformation

Tapping into your feelings allow you to connect with your soul.

How do you feel internally? How do you feel about yourself? Describe the emotions at this present moment.

_____

_____

_____

_____

_____

_____

_____

Being brutally honest will allow you to address the issues head-on without faking your smiles when deep down inside you are depressed. You allow yourself time to figure out what caused these feelings to occur. Embracing your vulnerability will allow you to feel free in a healthy state of being a hue-man.

Quick Personal Inventory Check	**Yes**	**No**
Place a check mark under yes or no		
Are you angry?	☐	☐
Are you lonely?	☐	☐
Do your thoughts match your feelings?	☐	☐
Are your shoulders tightened?	☐	☐
Do you have short breaths?	☐	☐
Are you rested?	☐	☐
Are you feeling inspired?	☐	☐
Do you feel cheerful?	☐	☐

LEAVE A REVIEW AND PURCHASE OTHER BOOKS DIRECTLY ON WWW.SHERIKADUNCAN.COM

THE SETUP NOVEL

SOUL YOU BOOK COLLECTION

Soul You Vol I: The Grand Awakening

Soul You Vol. II: The Procreator

Soul You Vol III: The Protector

Soul You Vol. IV: Scribble Journal

media@sherikaduncan.com

Copyright © 2021 Sherika Duncan Enterprise

All rights reserved.

www.ingramcontent.com/pod-product-compliance
Lightning Source LLC
Chambersburg PA
CBHW070052120526
44589CB00034B/2009